# RAY BRADBURY

Legendary Fantasy Writer

> " I followed my love: my love of adventure
> stories and comics and the possibilities of
> space travel and movies and dinosaurs and
> magic. " — Ray Bradbury

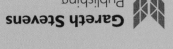
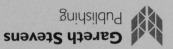

**Gareth Stevens**
Publishing

By Charles Piddock

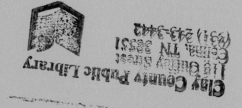
# RAY BRADBURY
## Legendary Fantasy Writer

*Life Portraits*

Please visit our web site at www.garethstevens.com.
For a free catalog describing Gareth Stevens Publishing's list of high-quality books, call 1-800-542-2595 (USA) or 1-800-387-3178 (Canada).
Gareth Stevens Publishing's fax: 1-877-542-2596

**Library of Congress Cataloging-in-Publication Data**
Piddock, Charles.
    Ray Bradbury: legendary fantasy writer / by Charles Piddock.
        p. cm. — (Life portraits)
    Includes bibliographical references and index.
    ISBN-10: 1-4339-0059-9   ISBN-13: 978-1-4339-0059-4 (lib. bdg.)
    1. Bradbury, Ray, 1920  2. Authors, American—20th century—Biography.
3. Science fiction, American—History and criticism. I. Title.
PS3503.R167Z84   2009
813'.54—dc22
    [B]                                                      2008031596


This edition first published in 2009 by
**Gareth Stevens Publishing**
A Weekly Reader® Company
1 Reader's Digest Rd.
Pleasantville, NY 10570-7000 USA

Copyright © 2009 by Gareth Stevens, Inc.

Executive Managing Editor: Lisa M. Herrington
Creative Director: Lisa Donovan
Cover Designer: Keith Plechaty
Interior Designers: Yin Ling Wong and Keith Plechaty
Publisher: Keith Garton

Produced by Spooky Cheetah Press
www.spookycheetah.com
Editor: Stephanie Fitzgerald
Designer: Kimberly Shake
Cartographer: XNR Productions, Inc.
Proofreader: Jessica Cohn
Indexer: Madge Walls, All Sky Indexing

Printed in the United States of America

1 2 3 4 5 6 7 8 9 12 11 10 09 08

# TABLE OF CONTENTS

*Traveling carnivals were very popular in the Midwest in the 1930s when Ray was growing up. People flocked to see the unusual attractions under the tents.*

## CHAPTER ONE

# MR. ELECTRICO

O N A LATE AFTERNOON IN SEPTEMBER 1932, A little 12-year-old boy with blond hair and glasses sat perched on the edge of a wooden bench. The flaps of the sideshow tent fluttered in the wind as the rows of benches filled up behind him. The boy shuffled his feet in the sawdust-covered floor, anxiously waiting for the show to begin. Some kids came to the Dill Brothers Combined Shows carnival to ride the carousel or make themselves sick on candy and snacks. Not this kid. Ray Bradbury came for the performers.

Every summer, the Dill Brothers carnival came to Waukegan, Illinois—Ray's hometown. For kids living in the early part of the 20th century, carnivals offered the prospect of almost unimaginable fun, thrills, and excitement. Ray looked forward to the arrival of the carnival more than anything else during the year—even Christmas.

A hush fell over the crowd as the curtain parted. Mr. Electrico, a magician, was sitting in an electric chair—the kind, the audience was assured, that was used to execute convicted killers. Suddenly, Mr. Electrico's assistant broke the silence by yelling, "Here go ten million volts of pure fire, ten million volts into the flesh of Mr. Electrico!"

The assistant pulled the lever on the electric chair, and a giant charge zapped through Mr. Electrico's body. Surely such a shock would have killed a lesser man, but Mr. Electrico simply smiled.

## Traveling Carnivals

Traveling carnivals are amusement shows that move from place to place, usually through small town and rural America. They were a popular feature of American life during the 19th century. Their heyday was during the Depression years of the late 1920s and early 1930s, when Ray was a young boy. Traveling carnivals were made up of amusement rides, food vendors, games of chance, thrill acts, animal acts, and sideshow curiosities, including magicians such as Mr. Electrico. Early traveling carnivals also included "freak shows." These featured bearded women, unusually tall or short people, or people with other deformities designed to shock and amaze viewers. Ray kept many of these images in his mind and later came to include some of them in his stories.

His white hair stood straight up and sparks shot out from his teeth. Mr. Electrico raised a heavy sword over the heads of the children in the audience, causing their hair to stand straight up. Then he approached the blond boy in the front row. Taking the electrified sword, Mr. Electrico tapped each of Ray's shoulders, his forehead, and the tip of his nose. "Live forever!" he cried.

## A MYSTERIOUS CONNECTION

Ray was thrilled and puzzled. Why had Mr. Electrico chosen him? The magician hadn't said anything to the other children. The next day, Ray went back to the carnival. He found Mr. Electrico sitting outside a tent. Looking for an excuse to talk to the mysterious magician, Ray asked him to figure out a toy magic trick he had in his pocket. After explaining the trick, the magician invited Ray to meet some of the other carnival folk. He introduced the boy to trapeze performers, dwarfs, a giant, the fat lady, and the illustrated man, who was covered with tattoos.

A while later, Mr. Electrico took Ray to the shore of Lake Michigan. He sat the boy down and began to explain why he had singled Ray out in his performance the day before. He said:

> *We've met before. You were my best friend [in World War I] in France in 1918, and you died in my arms in the battle of the Ardennes Forest that year. And here you are again, in a new body, with a new name. Welcome back!*

Mr. Electrico apparently believed that souls from past lives could be reborn again in new bodies. Ray was thunderstruck. He believed something amazing had happened to him. He was

> **"I decided that [the idea of living forever] was the greatest idea I had ever heard. Just weeks after Mr. Electrico said this to me, I started writing every day. I never stopped."**
>
> – RAY BRADBURY

fascinated by the idea that he had lived another life before—and that he would live forever. "I decided that [the idea of living forever] was the greatest idea I had ever heard," he later explained. "Just weeks after Mr. Electrico said this to me, I started writing every day. I never stopped."

Many years later, Ray tried to find out what had happened to Mr. Electrico. Strangely, no one could find any evidence that the man ever existed. Ray was unable to find any written accounts of the Dill Brothers Combined Shows, either. Yet he swears that the story is true and that it changed his life. If it is true, the modern world owes a huge debt to Mr. Electrico.

## A WRITER FOR THE AGES

Ray Bradbury has shaped our modern imagination perhaps more than any other popular writer. Ray's fans run in the millions. He has published more than 500 short stories, novels, plays, screenplays, television scripts, and poems. His best known and most beloved books, *The Martian Chronicles*, *The Illustrated Man*, *Fahrenheit 451*, and *Something Wicked This Way Comes*, are classic pieces of literature. His writing appeals to audiences young and old and has made him one of the great authors of the 20th century—as well as the 21st century and beyond. Ray Bradbury's storytelling skills have inspired generations and will continue to do so for years to come. In that sense, Mr. Electrico was right. Ray Bradbury certainly will live forever. As movie director Steven Spielberg said:

> *Ray Bradbury's most significant contribution to our culture is showing us that the imagination has no foreseeable boundaries. His skills as a storyteller have inspired and empowered generations to tell their stories no matter how bizarre or improbable. Today we need Ray Bradbury's gifts more than ever, and his stories have made him immortal.* ❖

*Ray's contributions to the motion picture industry earned him a star on the Hollywood Walk of Fame in 2002. Actors Rod Steiger (left) and Charlton Heston (right) were on hand to celebrate.*

*When Ray was a kid in the 1930s, Waukegan, Illinois, was a bustling town on the shore of Lake Michigan.*

## CHAPTER TWO

# A BOY'S LIFE

A S FAR AS ANYONE KNOWS, AT 4:50 P.M. ON August 22, 1920, no Martians landed on Earth. No time travelers arrived. No strange creatures climbed up from the bottom of Lake Michigan. What did arrive that summer day was one of the greatest imaginations of our time. That was the time and day Ray Douglas Bradbury was born in Waukegan, Illinois, a then-bustling town just north of Chicago.

Ray claims to remember every detail of his birth, from the darkness of the womb to the bright light of the hospital room. He swears this is true, even though psychologists say it is impossible. Ray, who was born one month late, claims his extra time in the womb made it possible for him to remember everything. "When you stay in the womb for ten months, you develop your eyesight and your hearing," he explained. "So when I was born, I remember it."

## DEEP AMERICAN ROOTS

Ray's family tree had deep roots in America. First to come to the New World was Thomas Bradbury. He left England for the Massachusetts Bay Colony in 1634. Thomas became a prominent member of the colony, but his wife, Mary Bradbury, really made history. On July 26, 1692, she was charged with witchcraft. Several witnesses claimed she had changed herself into a wild pig that caused a horse to throw its rider. Said witness Richard Carr: "I saw Mrs. Bradbury go into her gate, turn the corner of, and immediately there darted out of her gate a blue boar."

### The Salem Witch Trials

The Salem Witch Trials took place between May and October 1692 in the Massachusetts Bay Colony. In February and March of that year, two young girls began having fits and seeing visions. They claimed they were possessed by the devil and accused three Salem women of witchcraft. The women were pressured by authorities to accuse others of witchcraft. False confessions and hysteria spread across the colony. Officials set up a special court in Salem to try the accused. The trials resulted in the conviction of 19 "witches," including Mary Bradbury, and the imprisonment of 150 others. The trials were stopped by October and later denounced. The colonial legislature eventually overturned all the convictions.

*The home in which Ray and his brother grew up was not the largest house in Waukegan, but it was cozy and comfortable.*

Another charge brought against Mary was that she appeared as an apparition (ghost) aboard a ship bound for Barbados. On September 6, 1692, she was found guilty and sentenced to die. Thomas bribed the guards so she could escape prison.

Ray's great-great-grandfather was the first Bradbury to move west. He settled in Waukegan in 1847. Ray's father, Leonard, was born there in 1890. That was the same year that Ray's mother, Esther Marie Moberg, moved to America from Sweden with her family. Ray's parents were married in 1914. On July 17, 1916, Esther gave birth to twin boys: Leonard Jr., later called "Skip," and Sam. Sam died from the Spanish flu when he was only 2 years old.

## EARLY INFLUENCES

Esther was still mourning the loss of her baby when Ray was born in 1920. She vowed to keep her new child safe at all costs. As a result, little Ray was very sheltered. Mrs. Bradbury never let him far from her sight. When she did the laundry, Esther would take a rope and tether Ray to an apple tree so he could not crawl away. Ray drank from a bottle until he was 6 years old. His mother fed him with a spoon until he was nearly 12. Ray was safe, but he was a fearful child. He had many nightmares.

Ray attributes his lifelong fascination with scary and strange things to those early years of his life. "I have a feeling my mother infected me," he says. "She was a very fearful woman. I think a

*Lon Chaney (1883–1930) was one of America's greatest screen actors. His portrayal of Quasimodo in the 1923 silent film* The Hunchback of Notre Dame *sparked the imagination of 3-year-old Ray Bradbury.*

lot of her fears were transferred over to me. She was afraid something might happen to me."

Even though he dealt with fears and nightmares, Ray was not a shy or solitary child. He was very sociable and loved to be the center of attention.

"He used to play out in the yard in the dirt," recalled Edna Hutchinson, who later married Ray's uncle. "He had a spoon and when I would walk by, he would say 'Look!' and he would take a spoonful of dirt and eat it."

> **"[Ray] used to play out in the yard in the dirt. He had a spoon and when I would walk by ... he would take a spoonful of dirt and eat it."**
>
> – EDNA HUTCHINSON

Ray's mother also influenced him in positive ways. Esther loved the movies, and she passed that love on to her son. Since her husband didn't like to go to the theater, Esther took Ray to see the latest movies. To this day, he remembers when, as a 3-year-old, he saw silent film star Lon Chaney in *The Hunchback of Notre Dame*:

> *The Hunchback appealed in some secret way to something inside me which made me feel at the age of three, impossible as it seems, that perhaps I was some sort of Hunchback myself ... Chaney was so incredible at doing his portrayal and his lost love was so touching and immediate that my whole soul went forward at that young age and, it seems amazing that in my small body, I would crouch down inside myself and become the Hunchback, but that's what happened.*

Ray's aunt Neva Bradbury was also a big influence on the boy. In 1925, Aunt Neva gave Ray a Christmas present that he would come to treasure. It was *Once Upon a Time,* a book of timeless fairy tales including "Jack and the Beanstalk," "Snow White," "Tom Thumb," and others. His parents had been teaching 5-year-old Ray how to read. Now, through the book, he was able to plunge into a wonderful fantasy world. Ray loved the stories, but it was the beautiful illustrations by Margaret Evans Price that drew him to the book again and again.

> **"Now, when I go into a bookstore, I rush right to the children's section because of the illustrations."**
>
> – RAY BRADBURY

"Now, when I go into a bookstore," Ray said many years later, "I rush right to the children's section because of the illustrations." In fact, even with his own books, Ray was always very concerned with illustrations and book covers. He has even created the artwork for some of his book covers. Ray says this interest in illustrations can be traced back to his early love of *Once Upon a Time* and its artwork.

Neva, who was a teenager at the time, loved to read. She had a large collection of books, which included the *Oz* series by L. Frank Baum. Naturally, Neva shared her books with Ray. These classic stories about the adventures of Dorothy and her motley assortment of friends were like nothing the little boy had ever read before. As with the stories and pictures in *Once Upon a Time,* the *Oz* books transported Ray into a world of fantasy that he loved.

## HEADING WEST

In 1926, when Ray was in first grade, the Bradburys moved west. After a two-week stopover in Roswell, New Mexico, they settled in Tucson, Arizona. Leonard Bradbury always loved the American West. As a young man, Ray's father had worked in the gold fields of Nevada. Leo had not been able to strike it rich, so he headed back to Waukegan after less than a year. Ever since that time, he had dreamed of returning to the region.

Tucson couldn't have been more different than Waukegan. Ray's Illinois hometown was a lakefront community. It was sur-rounded by forests and ravines and crisscrossed by creeks. Not far from Waukegan were acres and acres of farmland. In Tucson, the land was hot and dry. It seemed like there wasn't so much as a blade of grass on the ground. Giant cacti grew everywhere. Ray loved this new setting. His mother felt comfortable there,

*Ray's parents, Esther and Leo, were incredibly proud of Ray's many literary accomplishments.*

too. She finally allowed Ray more freedom. He spent many afternoons roaming around the town and running wild on the University of Arizona campus. The only part of his old life that Ray missed was Aunt Neva, who was still in Waukegan.

Unfortunately, Leonard couldn't find work in Arizona. The family had to move back to Waukegan in the spring of 1927.

## MAGICAL TIMES

Ray was sad to leave the adventure of the desert and the friends he had made there. In keeping with his personality, though, he quickly found another fascination. In 1928, Ray was in the third grade. Decades later he still remembered being hypnotized

*Blackstone the magician (right) was a master of illusion. He was one of Ray's earliest heroes.*

## Blackstone the Magician

Harry Blackstone Sr. (1885–1965) was the most famous magician of his time. On stage, he often wore a top hat and tuxedo. He remained silent during his show, choosing to wow his audience without speaking. He performed dozens of illusions, but one of his most famous was the levitating woman. First, Blackstone had a young woman lie on a couch. He would cover her with a cloth, and then cause the entire couch to rise up into the air. When he pulled off the cloth—*poof*—the woman had disappeared! Another popular Blackstone illusion was to saw a woman in half. He used a large circular saw. As the blade appeared to pass through the woman's body, the audience heard a ripping sound and shrieks of pain. Of course, the woman rose unhurt at the end. The young Ray Bradbury saw Blackstone perform these illusions again and again. Like the rest of the audience, he was amazed each time he saw the tricks.

then by a large billboard on the back of the Academy Theater in Waukegan. The billboard advertised the coming of Blackstone the magician. Ray had recently become interested in magic. Like many other young boys, he dreamed about mystifying family and friends with his own magic tricks. Now he was going to get the chance to see the great Blackstone, perhaps the most amazing magician of the time!

*Ray spent many happy hours at the Waukegan public library as a young boy. He became a lifelong supporter of libraries and reading.*

"By the time Blackstone finally arrived in Waukegan for his first appearance, I was on the verge of a nervous breakdown," Ray remembers. Once the magician got to town, the youngster bought tickets for all his shows. He sat in the front row of the theater every time. The entire time Blackstone was in Waukegan, Ray rushed to the theater right after school. He was there in time to watch the afternoon matinees. He stayed until evening, watching back-to-back performances.

All Ray could think about was becoming a magician. He dreamed about being just like Blackstone. Ray spent hours scouring the Waukegan libraries for books on magic.

## FANTASY WORLDS

In the autumn of 1929, Ray's interest in magic gave way to a new fad. A new comic strip called *Buck Rogers in the 25th Century* appeared in the *Waukegan News*. It was the first science-fiction comic strip ever, and Ray loved it. He began cutting the strips out of the paper and collecting them. Ray talked constantly about Buck to his schoolmates and friends. He was obsessed, and the other kids teased him until it hurt. They asked what the point of collecting *Buck Rogers* comic strips could possibly be. "There aren't going to be any rocket ships," they said. "We aren't ever going to land on Mars or the Moon."

Ray was very sensitive; his friends' words hurt. Eventually they convinced him that they were right. He realized that there *weren't* going to be any rocket ships or Moon landings. One afternoon Ray rushed home from school and tore up the entire collection. Years later, he still regretted what he had done. "My *Buck Rogers* collection!" Ray said. "[It was] like giving away my head, my heart, my soul, and half a lung. I walked wounded for a year after that. I grieved and I cursed myself for having so dumbly tossed aside what was, in essence, the greatest love of my life. Imagination. Romance. Intuition. Love."

> "My *Buck Rogers* collection! ... I walked wounded for a year after that. I grieved and I cursed myself for having so dumbly tossed aside what was, in essence, the greatest love of my life. Imagination. Romance. Intuition. Love."
>
> – RAY BRADBURY

In 1930, Ray discovered yet another imaginary world. His Uncle Bion Bradbury loved the adventure stories of Edgar Rice Burroughs. When Ray went to visit, his uncle showed him Burroughs's novels about Mars. Novels such as *A Princess of Mars, The Gods of Mars,* and *The Warlords of Mars* fired the young boy's imagination. Twenty years later they would provide the inspiration for Ray to write his own book about the Red Planet. In the summer of 1930, it was Burroughs's *Tarzan of the Apes* that really captured Ray's imagination. For awhile Ray went "*Tarzan* crazy." Years later he remembered:

> *At breakfast I climbed trees for my father, stabbed a mad gorilla for my brother, and entertained my mother with pithy sayings right smack-dab out of Jane Porter's mouth. My father got to work earlier each day. My mother took aspirin for precipitant migraine. My brother hit me.*

## SNAKES AND GILA MONSTERS

By 1932, when Ray was still swinging from imaginary jungle trees and battling bad guys in space, the reality of the Great Depression (1929–1939) hit home. Leo lost his job at the Bureau of Power and Light. The Bradburys packed up their possessions, piled into their 1928 Buick, and were on their way back to Arizona. After nine days on Route 66, the dust-covered vehicle rolled into downtown Tucson. School had already begun by the time the Bradburys arrived in Arizona in September. Ray was enrolled in seventh grade at Amphitheater Junior High, and Skip started 11th grade.

## Me Tarzan

Tarzan is the most famous character invented by Edgar Rice Burroughs (1875–1950). In *Tarzan of the Apes* (the first book), readers are introduced to Tarzan as a baby. English Lord Greystoke and Lady Greystoke are marooned off the west coast of Africa. After they die, their infant son is adopted by apes and given the name Tarzan. (That means "white skin" in Burroughs's fictional ape language.) Tarzan grows up with the apes and learns the ways of the jungle. When he is 20 years old, Tarzan meets a young woman named Jane Porter. Like the baby Tarzan, Jane is marooned off Africa. Tarzan falls in love, and after Jane is rescued, he leaves the jungle to find her. In later books, Tarzan marries Jane, and they return to Africa, where they have a number of adventures. Burroughs went on to write 25 *Tarzan* books, which were wildly popular, mainly among young boys like Ray Bradbury. Tarzan also became the main character in a radio serial, a number of Hollywood movies, and a popular 1950s TV show.

Ray constantly talked about becoming a writer. Mr. Electrico had told Ray he would live forever. Ray felt he could accomplish that as a writer. After he was gone, his words would live on. For Christmas 1932, Leo and Esther bought their budding author a tin typewriter. He wrote every single day. He wrote *Tarzan* stories, original *Buck Rogers* scripts, and countless letters to his cousins and Aunt Neva.

Ray also developed a new obsession during this time—radio. Television had yet to come on the scene. During the Depression, radio was everyone's cheap entertainment.

To his delight, Ray discovered KGAR, a radio station that broadcast serials, just two blocks from his house. He began to visit the KGAR studio soon after the family arrived in Tucson. He offered to run errands for the crew and help out around the station for free. He hung around and pestered the employees so much that they finally gave him a chance to perform on the

## The Golden Age of Radio

From the early 1920s until the dawn of television in the 1950s, radio enjoyed a golden age in America. From coast to coast, music, news, and popular programs filled the airwaves. Radio was TV without the pictures. Popular shows included comedies, such as *The Burns and Allen Show* and *The Jack Benny Program*. There were adventure serials including *The Lone Ranger* and *Dick Tracy*. Programs such as *Suspense*, *Escape*, and *X-Minus One* offered radio plays filled with mystery, horror, and tales of the bizarre. Many of these shows adapted stories by famous writers. When Ray became a professional writer, his stories were adapted for some of his favorite radio shows.

*Even though he lived in Los Angeles, Ray (center) remained one of Waukegan's favorite sons. On June 27, 1990, the town named a park after him. Here, he poses with members of the parks department.*

air. Every Sunday children were given a chance to read newspaper comic strips on the radio. In the spring of 1933, 12-year-old Ray was asked to read comics such as *Tailspin Tommy, The Katzenjammer Kids,* and *Bringing Up Father* to kids listening all over southern Arizona.

Before long, though, Ray got some bad news. The family had to go back to Illinois. Leo had not been able to find a full-time job in Arizona. He had been selling homemade "chili-bricks," dried chili that could be cooked in boiling water, but it wasn't enough to support the family. In May 1933, the Bradburys packed up and headed back to Waukegan. ❖

*The Bradburys moved around a lot when Ray was young. Once the family settled in California in 1934, however, Ray knew he had found his home for life.*

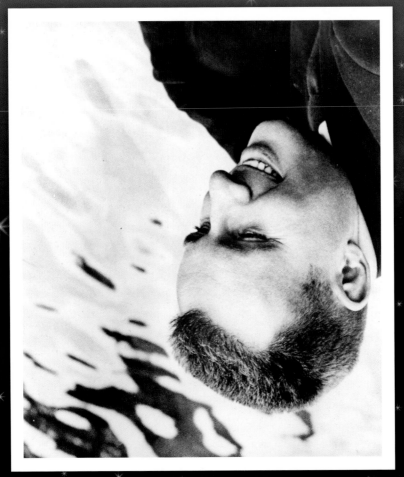

## CHAPTER THREE

# ADVENTURES IN HOLLYWOOD

B Y 1934, RAY WAS BACK IN WAUKEGAN. WHEN he wasn't in school, he could be found pounding away on his little typewriter, writing stories and letters. In his free time, Ray went to the movies and listened to his favorite programs on the radio.

That same year, Ray's Uncle Inar moved with his family to California. He sent postcards and letters to Ray's family back in Waukegan. Every time he wrote, Inar talked about the wonderful climate in California and the seemingly endless sunny days. He seemed to end every letter by suggesting that Leo, Esther, Ray, and Skip come west, too.

By the spring of 1934, Leo didn't need much persuading. He had been laid off from the power company where he worked. Once again, he loaded up the family in the old Buick. This time, however, they headed for Los Angeles. Ray, of course, was

*Ray knew he wanted to be a writer from the time he was a little kid. Though he was mainly interested in fantasy, Ray joined the poetry club in high school.*

delighted. To him, Los Angeles meant Hollywood—and Hollywood meant the movies. Ray couldn't believe his luck. He would actually be living right where all of his favorite movies were filmed.

The Bradbury family arrived in Los Angeles in May 1934. Almost immediately, Ray strapped on his roller skates and skated a few blocks to the nearest movie studio, which happened to be Paramount. From that moment on, the autograph hound became a fixture outside the studio.

Ray was relentless in his search for signatures. From the balcony of his family's apartment, he could see the rooftop of the Uptown Theatre, where the premieres of many new movies took place. Every time a new movie opened—which was about once a week—a red light on the top of the building would be turned on. Whenever Ray saw that red light shining, he would skate down to the theater and watch the stars arrive for their films. He was not shy about pestering his movie idols for their autographs.

## HIGH SCHOOL DAYS

In 1935, Ray was a sophomore at Los Angeles High School. He was still writing every day, still a fan of radio and the movies, and now dreaming of becoming a screenwriter or an actor. He got good grades in English and in art classes, but he failed terribly in mathematics. He made best friends with another star-struck teen, Donald Harkins, and the two roamed all over Hollywood looking for autographs.

The outgoing teen found himself in trouble with a bully at school. Ray explained how it started:

> I was a [smart mouth]. I was in history class and the teacher asked a question and this Armenian boy sitting in front of me gave the answer and under my breath, I said 'Good guess.' And the teacher heard that and she said to the boy, 'Was that a guess?' Like a [darn] fool, he said, 'Yes.' So he got a zero and he started beating up on me. Every time he saw me, he would hit me on the arm. My arm was a series of bruises for years.

One fall afternoon during his junior year, Ray saw something that would spark a much grimmer recollection for years to come. A car carrying four people had been involved in a horrible accident. When Ray arrived on the scene, three people were dead. One woman was alive, but just barely. She looked at Ray as he stood over her. The moment they made eye contact, the woman died. "It was a scene out of a nightmare," Ray recalled.

> "It was a scene out of a nightmare. I stumbled home that day, barely able to walk. I had to hold on to trees and walls I was so stunned."
>
> – RAY BRADBURY

"I stumbled home that day, barely able to walk. I had to hold on to trees and walls I was so stunned." The accident scarred Ray so badly that he never learned how to drive a car. For the rest of his life he would walk or ride a bicycle around town. When necessary, Ray relied on others to drive. "About once a month," he admitted in a recent interview, "I still have nightmares about that poor woman who looked up at me."

## PURSUING HIS DREAM

Ray tried to forget about the horrible car crash by focusing on his writing. He had wanted to be a professional writer since he was 12 years old. More than anything, the teenager wanted to write scripts for movies and radio. Every day in typing class, Ray would write a new script for *The Burns and Allen Show*. The program, which starred real-life married couple George Burns and Gracie Allen, was one of the most popular on radio at the time. Every day after school, Ray would skate down to the studio where the show was produced and give his script to George Burns.

"[Burns] told me I was a genius and the scripts were brilliant," Ray remembers. "Of course they were lousy and he knew

# Burns & Allen

George Burns and Gracie Allen started performing together in the 1920s. They made one of the most successful transitions from vaudeville to radio of any performers. (Vaudeville shows were live variety shows that featured comedy teams like Burns and Allen, as well as singers and other performers.) After a decade in vaudeville, George and Gracie performed together for 18 years on radio and 10 years on TV. At first, they simply moved their vaudeville routine from the stage to the airwaves. When ratings began to slip in the 1940s, Burns decided to turn the show into a situation comedy. For the first time, he and Gracie (who were married in real life) played a married couple on the air. No matter the format, the core of the show was the same: Gracie's lovable scatterbrain was one of the most popular characters on radio and television.

*George Burns and Gracie Allen were one of the most popular comedy teams in history. Burns gave Ray Bradbury his first break in show business.*

that but was polite." Burns, however, did take one of Ray's jokes and use it in an episode that aired on February 26, 1936.

When Ray heard the words he had written on the radio, it was like a shot of adrenaline for his dreams. He wanted to write, direct, and act in radio and the movies. He wanted it as much as he ever wanted anything.

As a child Ray lived in Waukegan, Illinois, and Tucson, Arizona, before settling permanently in California.

He'd had his first real "break" in comedy, but Ray mostly wrote science fiction. Although he had outgrown his old toy typewriter, Ray still didn't have a real one. Every day he gave up his lunch hour and rushed to the school's typing room to write stories. He typed furiously and, on average, was completing one story a week.

In his junior year, Ray enrolled in a poetry class at school and joined a poetry club. Both the class and the club were led by one of his favorite teachers, Snow Longley Housh. He also took a short-story course taught by Jennet Johnson. Both teachers saw something in the often brash teenager. On one of his early science-fiction stories, Johnson wrote, "I don't know what it is you're doing, but don't stop." Those words boosted Ray's confidence to sky-high levels. He was certain he would make a name for himself as a great American writer. ❖

*Ray always knew that he wanted to be a professional writer. He opted to use the library to further his education rather than attend college.*

## CHAPTER FOUR

# THE SCIENCE FICTION LEAGUE

I N THE FALL OF 1936, RAY SPOTTED A HANDBILL hanging in a secondhand bookstore. It advertised a local group called the Science Fiction League. Ray had been writing science fiction and was interested in anything related to the field. The meeting was to be held Thursday night upstairs at Clifton's Cafeteria. Nothing could keep him away.

At his first meeting, Ray sat sipping a milk shake as he looked around at the group. Like him, the people in the room were all unknowns at the time. However, there were several people who later became famous science-fiction authors. Jack Williamson was there. So was Robert Heinlein. Forrest J. Ackerman, one of the founders of the league, later made his name as a literary agent to science-fiction writers. Nevertheless, Ray stood out. Ackerman remembered his first impression of the teen, who was always talking and liked to imitate the voices of famous people—

even when his listeners were tired of hearing them. "Ray was a rather boisterous young boy," Ackerman said. "It's a wonder we didn't strangle him."

Young Ray was befriended by helpful and imaginative writers. Members of the league discussed one another's work and tried to help other members get published. They scheduled lectures on science and writing. The group also published its own magazine, called *Imagination!* In January 1938, Ray published his first short story, a tale of horror titled "Hollerbochen's Dilemma," in *Imagination!* The 17-year-old author was overjoyed.

Six months later, Ray graduated from Los Angeles High School. He knew he didn't want to go to college. He wanted to be a writer and felt he was well on his way. Ray didn't think he would learn more in college than he could teach himself. Instead of getting another degree, he vowed to educate himself through L.A.'s public library system. He planned to go to a library to study several times a week.

> **"Ray was a rather boisterous young boy. It's a wonder we didn't strangle him."**
>
> – FORREST J. ACKERMAN

Before he could start his study program, however, Ray had to find a job to help support his family. It didn't take long. In August, a former classmate who sold newspapers on a street corner offered to sell his post to Ray for $80. Ray borrowed the money from his father and brother. Soon he was a salesman for *The Herald Express*. Ray worked five afternoons a week from 4:00 to 6:30. That left him most of the day and weekends to write stories on a new typewriter he had bought.

## A Born Salesman

A fellow newspaper salesman at the time, Bob Gorman, recalled working near Ray. "He was aggressive and outward and very sociable as a salesman," Gorman said. "He worked hard. He was real easy to talk to. He talked a lot about when he would go to Hollywood and the people he would meet. The stars." Gorman also recalled that when Ray was not selling newspapers, he was almost always on his roller skates.

## NEW YORK BOUND

In the summer of 1939, Ray took a break from his job and his studies and took a trip to the opposite coast. The first World Science Fiction Convention was being held in New York on July 2 and 3. Nothing like this had been held before, and science-fiction fans all over the country were excited about it. When Ray heard about the convention, he was determined to go. He borrowed bus fare from Ackerman and boarded a Greyhound headed for New York.

The convention marked a moment in the growth of American science fiction. Until that point, sci-fi fans (a majority of whom were teenage boys) had corresponded mainly by mail. Now they had the chance to get together in one place. Some wore Buck Rogers outfits and other costumes of the 25th century. Others came dressed as characters from H. G. Wells's science-fiction story "Things to Come." Fame was to come for some of the attendees. Williamson, from the Science Fiction League, made the trip. So did the young Isaac Asimov. Williamson ultimately produced more than 50 science-fiction books. Asimov went on to write dozens of best-selling books. His short story "Nightfall" is considered by many to be the finest science-fiction short story ever written. Ray Bradbury, who sometimes felt himself an outsider—alone in his imaginative world—no longer felt so alone.

## Science-Fiction Conventions

Ray didn't know it at the time, but by attending the first ever science-fiction convention, he was witnessing the birth of a phenomenon. Today, sci-fi and fantasy conventions are incredibly popular and have become big business. They even attract big stars that are connected with television series, such as *Battlestar Galactica*, or movies such as *Star Wars*. Some conventions are general and cover a whole area of sci-fi or fantasy. Others are specific to a particular show, movie, or character. Fans come to hear lectures, collect autographs, and buy gear modeled after the show, movie, or book. They also get the chance to mingle with other fans, many of whom come dressed in costume. It is estimated that nearly every weekend of the year there are at least two science-fiction or fantasy conventions taking place somewhere on Earth.

*Ray never lost his love for science-fiction and fantasy conventions. Many fans that attended the 2007 Comic-Con were lucky enough to meet the author.*

Ray spent a lot of time at the science-fiction convention, but he made time to see the famous landmarks in New York City. He also traveled to Long Island for the 1939 World's Fair. The fair was the largest ever presented. Sixty foreign governments had separate exhibits. Before the fair closed in 1940, 44 million people had visited.

The theme of the fair was "The World of Tomorrow." Some of its most popular exhibits included the first televisions, futuristic cars, and the first electric typewriters. Ray was in heaven. "I visited the fair with a group of my science fiction friends and I was entranced," he said. "I never wanted to leave." The vacation came to an end, however. By August, he was back in L.A.

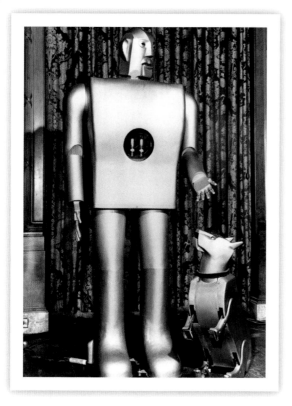

*Ray visited the Westinghouse exhibit at the 1939 World's Fair, which featured Electro and Sparko, a robot man and his dog. The exhibit was designed to show off the wonders of science and future technologies.*

## BREAKING INTO THE PULPS

Once Ray returned home, he didn't waste any time getting to work. He was more determined than ever to break into the "big time" of science-fiction writing. Then, on September 1, 1939, something happened that made him think he might have to put his writing career on hold. The news came over the radio that Germany had invaded Poland. World War II (1939–1945) had begun. The United States was not involved in the war—yet. But in the back of his mind Ray worried that he might someday be drafted and sent to fight. For the moment, he redoubled his efforts to launch his professional writing career.

Ray's efforts paid off in 1940. He wrote a short story called "It's Not the Heat, It's the Hu…" about a man who can't stand clichés. Ray submitted the piece to *Script*, a Hollywood literary magazine. Less than a week later, he received a letter from the magazine's editors. He ripped open the envelope in a flash. He could hardly believe his eyes. *Script* wanted to publish his story. It was Ray's first sale as a writer! He didn't get paid any money; he only received three free copies of the magazine. Still, Ray was overjoyed. He was now a professional writer.

## Pulp Magazines

Pulp magazines were inexpensive fiction magazines that were popular in the early part of the 20th century. Most were sold for ten cents a copy. The term *pulp magazine* came from the cheap newsprint paper on which they were printed. The magazines' peak popularity came in the 1920s and 1930s, when successful pulps could sell up to one million copies per issue. Among the best-known pulps were *Adventure*, *Amazing Stories*, *Dime Detective*, and *Weird Tales*. Many classic science-fiction and crime novels first came out in the pulps. These magazines kept costs down by paying writers less than slick magazines did. Many famous authors besides Ray Bradbury got their start writing for the pulps, including Raymond Chandler, Isaac Asimov, Zane Grey, and Jack London.

*After his first story was accepted by Super Science Stories in 1941, that magazine and other pulps began regularly publishing Ray's work. He soon became known as "the poet of the pulps."*

In 1941, Henry Hasse, one of Ray's friends in the writers' group, helped him plot "Pendulum." When it was finished, they sent the short story to Julius Schwartz, a New York agent for the pulps. Ray had been submitting stories to Schwartz since 1939. So far, the agent had turned down all of them. This time, however, Schwartz took the bait. On July 28, he sold Ray's story to *Super Science Stories,* a science-fiction magazine.

Ray was paid $27.50 for the story, which he split with Hasse. The pay wasn't great, but Ray was elated. He had arrived as a pulp writer. The issue of *Super Science Stories* with Ray's story hit the newsstands on August 22, 1941—the author's 21st birthday. Ray went back to his typewriter with renewed zeal.

## WAR THREATENS

On December 7, however, everything changed for Ray—and for all Americans. Japanese forces bombed the American naval base at Pearl Harbor, Hawaii. The country was at war. Leo and Esther Bradbury were worried that their boys would be drafted and sent to fight. Skip wanted to go; Ray didn't. He wasn't unpatriotic, but Ray had a feeling that if he went to war, he would never make it home. As it turned out, both Skip and Ray failed their draft physicals. Skip had a broken eardrum, and Ray's eyesight was so bad that he was disqualified from serving.

Ray turned to his writing with renewed energy. He made a pledge to write one story a week, every week, for a year. The technique worked. Schwartz, who was now his agent, sold two of Ray's stories to *Captain Future* magazine. At the end of 1942, after selling a number of stories to the pulps, Ray felt he was securely in his element. He quit his job selling newspapers and dedicated himself to a career as a professional writer. ❖

In the 1940s, Ray emerged as a major American writer. He was moving from the pulps to the mainstream.

## CHAPTER FIVE

# HITTING THE BIG TIME

B Y 1944, RAY WAS STILL WRITING A STORY A week. He had sold 22 sci-fi and fantasy stories in two years, and he was a star in the pulp universe. Some people were even calling him "the poet of the pulps" because his stories seemed to have a literary quality a cut above the rest.

In 1945, August Derleth, the publisher of Arkham House, contacted Ray. He wanted to publish a collection of Ray's fantasy fiction. Ray couldn't have been happier. He began compiling some of his stories into a book to be called *Dark Carnival*. The title comes from Ray's days of wandering carnival grounds and his meeting with Mr. Electrico. Published in 1947, *Dark Carnival* was Ray's first book.

Meanwhile, Ray continued writing new and original stories for magazines. He had "made it" in the pulps. His next challenge was getting published in the slick literary magazines.

Throughout 1945, Ray asked his agent to submit his stories to those magazines. Schwartz declined. He knew the pulp market, but did not have a lot of experience with the high-end market. The agent thought Ray might be better off trying to submit the stories on his own. Bradbury agreed to try, but he was worried that his success with the pulps might actually work against him. Ray felt that his name was too closely connected to the cheap magazines to gain acceptance from other kinds of magazines. He decided to submit his stories under a pen name. Of course, there was a potential downside to the plan. Ray realized there was little hope that an unknown writer would get published in a well-regarded national magazine.

*By the mid-1940s, Ray's fame was growing. He was also starting to make a good living as a writer.*

In July 1945, Ray submitted three stories under the made-up name of William Elliott. He sent "Invisible Boy" to *Mademoiselle,* "The Miracles of Jamie" to *Charm,* and "One Timeless Spring" to *Collier's.* Just one month later, Ray received surprising news in the mail. The editors of all three magazines had written to accept his submissions. Today, Ray remembers that week as one of the happiest of his life. "I've never had a week like that since," he said. Ray was paid $1,000 for all three stories. That was twice as much as he would have earned in an entire year of selling newspapers!

## TRENCH COAT ROMANCE

One day in April 1946, Ray found a new type of success when he went to Fowler Brothers bookstore in downtown Los Angeles. Someone had been shoplifting books, and Ray looked like a likely suspect. It was a hot day, but he was wearing a long trench coat with deep pockets. One of the clerks began following him around the store. Her name was Marguerite McClure. At 24 years old, she was one year younger than Ray.

When Marguerite confronted Ray, he told her that he was looking for a book called *Who Knocks?* He said that one of his stories, called "The Lake," was included in the anthology. Later, Marguerite took a copy of the book home and read the story. "The Lake" is about a 12-year-old boy whose girlfriend drowned in the waters of Lake Michigan. Her body was never found. Years later, the boy, who is grown up and married, returns to the town. As he walks along the beach on a late summer day, the little girl from his past appears from the depths.

*Ray's interest in illustration started when he was a child. He remained very involved in the illustrations for his books—and even drew some himself.*

Marguerite was dazzled by the story. By this time, she'd decided that Ray might be a good catch! As it turns out, Ray was just as smitten with Marguerite as she was with him. He returned to the store a few days later and somehow found the courage to ask her out. Ray had been on one date before in his life, and that had been years before. Happily, Marguerite accepted. The two quickly fell in love and became engaged in June 1946.

Earlier that month, Ray had turned in a completed manuscript for *Dark Carnival*. "The Lake" made another appearance in that book, along with stories about magic, ghosts, vampires, and dreams. In "The Wind," Ray writes about a man who is convinced that the howling winds he hears at night mean to kill him. In "Uncle Einar," Ray tells the story of a lovable vampire with green wings. He wrote, in part:

*Uncle Einar's beautiful silklike wings hung like sea-green sails behind him and whirred and whispered from his shoulders when he sneezed or turned around swiftly.*

## MORE GOOD NEWS

Soon after *Dark Carnival* was published, Ray learned that his short story "The Big Black and White Game" was chosen to be included in *Best American Short Stories* of 1946. The story was about a baseball game between an all-white team and an all-black team.

Though Ray had gained great success in print, he never abandoned his desire to work in radio. He constantly submitted scripts to radio stations. In 1946, Ray wrote a one-act play for radio called "The Meadow." He submitted it to ABC's *World Security Workshop,* which was a drama program. ABC selected the script, and it aired on January 2, 1947. Ray sold a second script less than a year later. This was just the start of the author's long association with the medium. In addition to original works that were created for broadcast, many of Ray's short stories were later adapted for the airwaves.

Meanwhile, inclusion in *Best American Short Stories* exposed Ray's work to the top literary people in New York. By the summer of 1947 publishers were contacting him asking for submissions. Katharine S. White from *The New Yorker* was just one editor who asked Ray for a short story. "I See You Never," the story of a Mexican man deported to his homeland, ran in the November 8, 1947, issue. It had only taken a few years for "the poet of the pulps" to reach the nation's top literary magazine.

Ray also got more good news. Don Congdon offered to be his agent. Ray had worked with him when Congdon was an editor at the publishing house of Simon & Schuster. Ray always liked Congdon. He was overjoyed to have him as his agent.

In the meantime, Ray had married his sweetheart on September 27, 1947. They rented a one-bedroom apartment on Venice Boulevard. It was just a short distance from the beach and from Ray's parents' apartment. It didn't seem like things could get any better. However, 1948 brought even more opportunities.

## Sci-Fi on Radio

Radio, called "the theater of the imagination," was the perfect medium for science-fiction stories. Without the distraction of pictures, people could let the stories come to life in their minds. There were many programs that featured the works of the most popular science-fiction writers of the day. *Dimension X* was one of radio's best sci-fi programs. Over the years, several of Ray's works, including *The Martian Chronicles*, were performed on the show. Ray's works were also adapted for more mainstream programs, such as *Suspense*.

*In 1980,* The Martian Chronicles *was made into a television miniseries starring Rock Hudson (left).*

Ray's literary success continued to build. His short story "Powerhouse" was published in *Charm* magazine. The story is about a woman driving through the desert who takes shelter from a storm in a powerhouse. "Powerhouse" won third prize in the 1948 O. Henry Prize Story collection. That same year, "I See You Never" was included in *The Best American Short Stories.*

## BIRTH OF THE MARTIAN CHRONICLES

Even as he juggled all these projects, Ray continued to think about a book of short stories about Mars. He had never lost his boyhood fascination with the Red Planet. Ray wanted to put together a book about Mars, Martians, and the Earth people who finally invade and conquer their planet. He thought he would model the collection on *Winesburg, Ohio,* a book by Sherwood Anderson. The series of short stories would all connect.

In 1949, Ray presented an outline of a proposed Mars book to Doubleday editor Walter Bradbury (no relation). Ray decided that the story line tying all the Martian tales together would be Earth's attempt to colonize the Red Planet. He proposed to adapt stories he had already written and add new stories around that central theme. The action would revolve around the Earthlings' bringing all the problems of Earth—such as pollution, racism, and cruelty—to a new planet.

In Ray's vision, the Martians have a gentle and advanced civilization. They communicate through mental telepathy and live in fairy-like cities. But they are not equipped to handle the Earthling

## Winesburg, Ohio

Ray Bradbury read *Winesburg, Ohio* by Sherwood Anderson (1876–1941) as a teenager. The novel was written as a series of connected short stories, each with a different main character, plot, beginning, and end. The stories explore the loneliness and frustrations of the fictional inhabitants of the town of Winesburg. The one character that connects all the stories together is named George Willard. Each character from the different stories tells George a tale that illuminates small town life. The highly acclaimed book is considered Anderson's best work. Ray hoped to bring a Martian world to life just as Anderson had done with the fictional town of Winesburg.

*Ray never learned to drive a car. As a boy, he used roller skates to get around town. In later years, he enjoyed riding a bicycle.*

invasion. After turning back the first few rounds of humans, the Martians become ghosts haunting the planet.

Walter Bradbury liked the idea, and offered Ray a contract to write the book. Ray got right to work. Every day, he followed the same routine. He spent mornings at his typewriter. When it was time for lunch, Ray rode his bicycle over to his parents' house, where Esther made him an egg sandwich. At 2:00, he rode home to take a short nap. Then he would return to work on the book. Through the summer of 1949, Ray reviewed the two dozen Mars stories he had already published, deciding which ones to put into the book with new material.

The Mars of *The Martian Chronicles* is nothing like the real planet. It has an Earthlike atmosphere, with blue hills, trees, lawns, houses, and city plazas. Ray created a beautiful fantasy world for his Martians:

> *They had a house of crystal pillars on the planet Mars by the edge of an empty sea, and every morning you could see Mrs. K eating the golden fruits that grew from the crystal wall, or cleaning the house with handfuls of magnetic dust which, taking all dirt with it, blew away on the hot wind. Afternoons ... you could see Mr. K himself in his room, reading from a metal book with raised hieroglyphs over which he brushed his hand, as one might play a harp.*

Today we know enough about Mars to know Ray's version of the planet could not be possible. Even when he wrote the

*Ray considers himself a writer of fantasy and imagination—not science fiction. His visions often ignore scientific fact and go right to heart of the human imagination.*

story, scientists knew enough about Mars to know there were no homes made of crystal pillars. Ray has always seen himself as a fantasy writer, however, not a science-fiction writer bound by the facts of science. According to fellow writer Isaac Asimov, Ray "created his own version of Mars straight out of the 19th century, totally ignoring the findings of the 20th century."

> **"[Ray] created his own version of Mars straight out of the 19th century, totally ignoring the findings of the 20th century."**
>
> – ISAAC ASIMOV

In early October 1949, Ray sent the completed manuscript of *The Martian Chronicles* to Walter Bradbury in New York. Soon after, Ray and Marguerite's first child was born—a daughter named Susan Marguerite Bradbury. ❖

*Ray continued using a typewriter for story writing, even after computers came into use.*

# Sea Monsters and Illustrated Men

AFTER *THE MARTIAN CHRONICLES* WAS PUBLISHED, Ray continued to write a short story a week. The idea for one of his most famous stories was inspired by a walk he took with his wife, whom he called Maggie. Ray later recalled what he saw as they walked along the ocean and passed an old abandoned amusement park:

> *I was walking with Maggie one night on the beach as the fog rolled in and looked out and saw the old roller coaster lying over on its side with its bones in the sand and the water, and the wind blowing over its skeleton. I looked at it and said to Maggie, 'I wonder what that dinosaur is doing lying on the beach.'*

Later that night, Ray was awakened by the sound of a foghorn blaring. The writer says that almost at once, the idea for a story came to him. "The Foghorn" is about a dinosaur that had waited for a companion for millions of years in the dark depths of the sea. When it heard the foghorn blowing, the dinosaur thought it had found a mate. In the story, Ray described how, in a burst of expectation and joy, the lonely beast swam into the bay looking for its long-lost companion:

> … *then, from the surface of the cold sea came a head, a large head, dark-colored, with immense eyes, and then a neck. And then—not a body—but more neck and more! The head rose a full forty feet above the water on a slender and beautiful dark neck. Only then did the body, like a little island of black coral and shells and crayfish, drip up from the subterranean.*
>
> *… The fog horn blew.*
> *And the monster answered.*
> *A cry came across millions of years of water and mist. A cry so anguished and alone …*
> *The monster cried at the tower …*

When the monster discovers that the sound was not made by another dinosaur, it realizes that it is truly alone for all of eternity. The monster destroys the tower in anguish and despair, and then disappears forever into the depths of the cold, lonely sea. In "The Foghorn," Ray is able to use the power of language to make readers empathize with the lonely creature and its torment. No wonder critics loved the story and readers have read it over and over again for years.

*In 1979, Ray received a rare invitation to visit a control room of the National Aeronautics and Space Administration (NASA).*

Meanwhile, Ray began working on another book. Like *Dark Carnival,* this volume would feature a collection of short stories, some old and some new. The title Ray chose for the book was *The Illustrated Man.* The author selected some of his most powerful stories for the collection.

In "The Veldt" Ray warns readers about the dangers of technology. The story is about a family that buys a home with a high-tech nursery. In this room, dreams and fantasies come to life in the liquid crystal walls, ceiling, and floor. In the end, however, what sounds like the ultimate fantasy turns into a virtual-reality nightmare. When the parents threaten to lock up the room and turn off the entire house, the children—and the house—fight back. The results are cataclysmic.

Maggie was pregnant with the couple's second child when Ray was working on *The Illustrated Man*. Their living conditions were getting crowded, so they searched for more spacious housing. They found a house in West Los Angeles and moved in on August 3, 1950. Ray converted the garage into an office.

As *The Illustrated Man* neared completion, Ray wrote a prologue story to tie the other stories in the book together. It begins with a young man wandering the back roads of Wisconsin. He meets another wanderer, an unemployed carnival freak who is tattooed from head to toe. Of course these are no ordinary tattoos. The drawings come to life at night and predict horrible things. Each tattoo represents a short story in the book. *The Illustrated Man* was published on February 23, 1951, when Ray was only 30 years old. Just three months later, on May 17, 1951, his second daughter, Ramona Anne, was born.

## WRITING WITH A POLITICAL EDGE

Many of Ray's stories have a message or warning. "The Veldt" warns of the dangers of technology. *The Martian Chronicles* highlights the destructive nature of humans. Ray also had a way of transferring daily happenings or observations into fantasy, as he did in "The Foghorn."

As the 1950s dawned, Ray became increasingly worried about the political climate in the United States. Those were the years when the Cold War led to fears that communists had infiltrated America. There was a "red scare" that caused many people to suspect everyone else of being communists. The situation caused Ray great concern and began to influence his writings.

## The Cold War

The Cold War refers to a period of tension between the Soviet Union and the United States roughly between 1946 and 1989. It was called the Cold War because it never turned into an actual military conflict. The Cold War remained a battle of ideologies between the forces of communism, led by the Soviet Union, and the forces of democracy, led by the United States. During this period, both the United States and the Soviet Union built up large arsenals of nuclear weapons. This arms race led to tension and fear that the Cold War could, at any time, lead to a nuclear conflict and an end to civilization.

In the fall of 1951 Ray was walking home late at night with a friend when a police car pulled up beside them. The officer stepped out and asked what the men were doing.

"Putting one foot in front of the other," said Ray. Angered, the officer asked again what they were doing.

"Breathing the air," Ray answered this time, "talking, conversing, walking."

"Just walking?" the officer asked suspiciously. When Ray and his friend nodded the officer demanded, "Don't do it again!"

It was unusual to see people walking in Los Angeles. Most people who lived in the city drove their cars everywhere—no matter how short a distance they were covering. Still, there was

*In 1947, Hollywood's biggest stars were called to testify in front of a congressional committee investigating communism in the motion picture industry. Ray was very opposed to the hearings.*

no reason to suspect Ray and his friend were up to no good. Ray was furious at being stopped when he was obviously doing nothing wrong. The incident inspired him to go home and write "The Pedestrian." The story is about a future society in which walking is forbidden. All pedestrians are treated as criminals.

In October, Ray started work on a short novel with a similar theme. The story takes place in a future where books are considered dangerous and are burned. Ray was unable to make a good start on the book, though. He was having too much trouble concentrating in his garage office. It was noisy and too close to "home." Ray's little girls wanted to play with him during work hours, and he had trouble refusing. Quickly realizing that he needed a different workspace, Ray transferred his office to the Los Angeles public library, which had a typing room downstairs. Each typewriter had a timer and could be rented for ten cents per half hour. After nine days and innumerable dimes, Ray had a 25,000-word novel, which he called *The Fireman*. He didn't think the work was quite ready to be published, so Ray put the manuscript aside to concentrate on other projects.

Ray revisited *The Fireman* in late 1952. He signed an agreement with Ballantine Books to add another 25,000 words to the book. He continued working on the story until January 1953. That month Ray finished the novel, but he wasn't happy with the title. For several weeks he tried to come up with a new name, but wasn't having any luck. Then, suddenly, on January 22, inspiration struck. Ray decided to ask experts for help—but even that turned out to be more difficult than he'd anticipated. The author recalled:

> *I decided I might well use the temperature at which paper catches fire. I telephoned the chemistry department at several universities and found no one who could tell me the right temperature. I made inquiries, also, of several physics professors. Then, still ignorant, I slapped my forehead and muttered, 'Fool! Why not ask the fire department!'*
>
> *The fireman told me that book paper ignited at 451 degrees Fahrenheit. I reversed it to Fahrenheit 451 because I liked the sound of it.*

## HIGH PRAISE

*Fahrenheit 451* hit the bookstores on October 19, 1953. The public loved the book. It quickly garnered high praise from critics around the country. Orville Prescott, the book critic for *The New York Times*, wrote:

> *Mr. Bradbury's account of this insane world, which bears many alarming resemblances to our own, is fascinating … his basic message is a plea for … [the great value of books in our society to promote independent thinking and free thought].*

### Title Wars

When Michael Moore's documentary film *Fahrenheit 9/11* was about to hit the theaters in 2004, Ray Bradbury hit the ceiling. He accused Moore of taking the title from *Fahrenheit 451* and using it without permission. "Michael Moore is a screwed up [jerk]," he said. "He stole my title and changed the numbers without ever asking me for permission … [Moore] is a horrible human being." The documentary maker called Bradbury to apologize, but Ray was not satisfied. He wanted the film's title changed, but it was already too late. Ray never took any legal action against Moore. He wouldn't have had a case. It is not illegal to adapt a title from another work.

Fahrenheit 451 *proved to be Ray's most successful novel. In 2005, he joined a group of high school students in Long Beach, California, for a week-long event honoring the book.*

Fahrenheit 451 has gone on to become Ray's best-selling book. In 1966, it was made into a popular movie. The book has become a classic and is taught in high school English classes all over the country. Ray, who considers himself a fantasy writer, not a science-fiction writer, says that *Fahrenheit 451* is his only pure science-fiction book. ❖

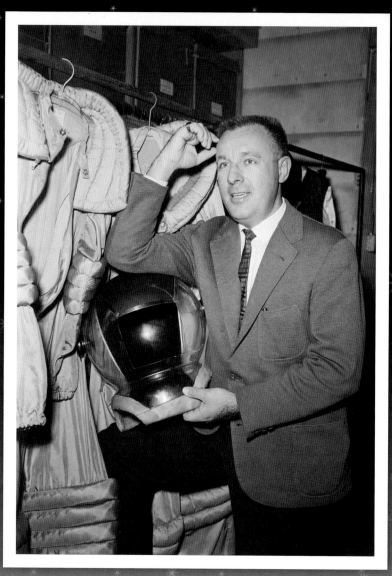

*Ray was always interested in adapting his stories for movies and TV. He liked to be involved in every aspect of the work—from scriptwriting to picking costumes.*

# MOVIE MADNESS

WITH THE PUBLICATION OF *FAHRENHEIT 451* in 1953, Ray established himself as an author with a wide and adoring audience. The critics loved him, and so did millions of readers. He had accomplished many of his dreams, yet Ray never gave up his burning desire to be involved in the movies.

The writer had met John Huston, his favorite movie director, in the 1950s. At the time, the director expressed an interest in making a movie from *The Martian Chronicles*. Huston was one of Ray's heroes. Ray wrote:

> [Huston] knew how to get actors to live inside the skin
> of their characters so you weren't watching actors acting,
> you were watching people living. When a director can do
> this, you forget that you are looking at a motion picture.

Soon after Ray finished *Fahrenheit 451,* he heard that Huston was visiting Los Angeles. He hoped the director would call him to talk about doing a screenplay, but days went by without any contact from Huston. Ray was about to give up hope.

## THE OPPORTUNITY OF A LIFETIME

On August 18, Maggie took a call from Huston. When Ray got home, she told him the director was expecting a call back the next morning. When Ray and Huston finally spoke, they set up a meeting for the next evening.

At the meeting, Huston asked Ray what he was doing the next year. "Not much, Mr. Huston. Not much," Ray replied.

"Well, Ray, how would you like to come live in Ireland and write the screenplay of *Moby Dick?*" Huston asked.

Ray replied that he had never even managed to read the book, but Huston didn't seem to mind.

"Well," he said, "why don't you go home tonight, read as much as you can, and come back tomorrow and tell me if you'll help me kill a white whale."

> **"Come back tomorrow and tell me if you'll help me kill a white whale."**
>
> – JOHN HUSTON

Ray left the meeting and bought a copy of Herman Melville's classic book. He stayed up all night reading. The next morning he met with Huston and accepted the job. Then panic set in. Huston wanted Ray in Ireland in three weeks. That would have been plenty of time if Ray were willing to get on an airplane, but he simply refused to fly. Ray didn't trust airplanes. Instead, Ray and his family

## Moby Dick

Herman Melville's 1851 novel tells about the adventures of a sailor named Ishmael and his voyage on the whaling ship *Pequod*. The crew is out to hunt whales, but Captain Ahab is focused on killing a specific whale, Moby Dick, a white whale of tremendous size. In a previous encounter, Moby Dick destroyed Ahab's boat and bit off his leg. Ahab is out for revenge, but things do not turn out the way he intends. The novel is an adventure story and more. It is also a story about good vs. evil, man vs. nature, and the destructive power of obsession. Many critics have called *Moby Dick* the best American novel ever written.

traveled across the United States by train. Once in New York, they boarded a boat to cross the Atlantic to Ireland. A new and exciting adventure was beginning for all of them. Ray was about to live a dream he'd had since his mother took him to see *The Hunchback of Notre Dame* when he was 3 years old. He was finally writing for the movies—and for his favorite director! But Ray's dream assignment would quickly turn into a nightmare.

## RAY'S WHITE WHALE

The Bradburys arrived in Ireland at the end of September 1953. Ray got to work immediately turning the book into a movie script. He worked all day, seven days a week. He found the first

*When Ray was hired to work on* Moby Dick *it seemed like a dream come true. Unfortunately, the job quickly turned into a nightmare.*

weeks of writing to be nerve-wracking. Ray thought the script was just not coming together. He felt trapped and powerless. For the first time in his life, Ray began to feel depressed. He feared that his work was no good. His confidence was shaken, and he was deeply afraid that he would disappoint his hero.

In early November 1953, Ray nervously presented the first 50 pages of his screenplay to Huston. "John," he said, "if you don't like what you read here today, I want you to fire me. I want you to send me home." Ray went upstairs at Huston's house to nervously await the verdict. Nearly an hour later, Huston called Ray from the bottom of the stairs, saying, "Ray, come down and finish the screenplay."

"I came down the stairs weeping," Ray recalled. "I so loved the man, I so loved the project. At that point, the burden was lifted from my shoulders. Up until then, I was suicidal. But after that day, it was gone."

Although Huston approved of the screenplay, he did not seem to think much of Ray. Their relationship fell apart. The director was macho, gruff, and had a mean streak. Ray, a self-described "wimp," was easily brought to tears and constantly sought approval. Huston took advantage of Ray's sensitive nature whenever he got the chance. He played jokes on Ray and made fun of his fear of flying. One afternoon, as they rode in a cab on the way to lunch, Huston humiliated Ray just for a laugh. He told the others in the cab that Ray "did not have his heart in the project." Ray was hurt. He couldn't understand why Huston would say such a thing. Even though the director said he was just kidding, Ray found himself on the verge of tears.

> **"I came down the stairs weeping. I so loved the man, I so loved the project. At that point, the burden was lifted from my shoulders. Up until then, I was suicidal. But after that day, it was gone."**
>
> – RAY BRADBURY

By January 1954, Maggie had had enough. She couldn't stand to watch Ray suffer at the hands of Huston any longer. She and the girls left Ireland. They would stay in Italy until the script was done. Ray remained behind

## John Huston

It is hard to imagine anyone as different from Ray Bradbury as John Huston (1906–1987). Huston was a tall, brash, hard-drinking macho man who loved danger, loved to hunt, and was married five times. He grew up in Los Angeles, dropped out of high school, and became a top amateur boxer in his teens. In his early 20s, Huston joined the Mexican Army. After returning to the United States, he took some acting jobs in Hollywood. He also started writing scripts for the movies and got his first chance to direct in 1941 with *The Maltese Falcon*. Huston went on to direct 41 films over 46 years. A good friend of his, actress Lauren Bacall, described Huston as

*John Huston was a very talented writer, actor, and director who eventually became a Hollywood legend. As Ray found out, however, he was also a very difficult man.*

"daring, unpredictable, maddening, and mystifying." These were all qualities that Ray experienced firsthand in Ireland while he was writing the script for *Moby Dick*.

in Ireland, being tormented by Huston and trying to finish the script. Then one night, things came to a head. At a dinner attended by Huston, Ray, and several other people, the director started insulting Ray's friends. Ray finally stood up to his hero. He yelled at him and told him to shut up. Huston was stunned—and angry. The director almost started a fistfight with Ray.

By March, Ray was finally finished with the screenplay. The ordeal was over. After spending some time in Italy together, the Bradbury clan returned to the United States in May 1954. On July 22, 1955, Maggie gave birth to a third daughter, Bettina Francion Bradbury.

*Moby Dick* premiered in Hollywood in June 1956. For the first time in his life, Ray would be attending a movie premiere as an invited guest! It was a dream come true. Unfortunately, Ray was too nervous to enjoy the experience. He was too worried about what everyone would think of the film. *Moby Dick* was officially released on June 27, 1956. The movie did well at the box office, but is not considered one of Huston's best films. ❖

*Ray loved writing for television series such as* Alfred Hitchcock Presents *and* The Twilight Zone.

## CHAPTER EIGHT

# THE SMALL SCREEN

A FTER HIS EXPERIENCE WITH JOHN HUSTON, Ray decided he needed a break from working on movies. He did continue to work in both radio and television, though. Radio drama was still big in the early- to mid-1950s as television was just beginning to take over the nation. Other writers adapted Ray's stories for radio shows such as ABC *Radio Workshop* and the CBS program *Suspense*.

In 1955, the producers of the television program *Alfred Hitchcock Presents* approached Ray to do a script for the show. He very happily agreed. His first script, "Shopping for Death," is a story about two retired insurance salesmen who test a theory that the hotter the temperature gets, the more likely people are to commit murder. Ray was paid $2,250 for the script, which was a lot of money at the time. That episode of *Alfred Hitchcock Presents* aired on January 29, 1956.

## Alfred Hitchcock

Sir Alfred Hitchcock (1899–1980) was born in London, England. Over a career that lasted more than 50 years, he became one of the most famous and influential directors in movie-making history. Some of his classic suspense films include *Psycho*, *Rebecca*, *The Birds*, and *Marnie*. Hitch, as he was known to friends, produced his popular TV series in the 1950s and 1960s. When he died in 1980, 600 people attended his funeral.

MR. HITCHCOCK

*Alfred Hitchcock was a talented director who was well-liked and respected by his peers.*

Ray liked the creative process of working on *Alfred Hitchcock Presents*. First he would meet with the producers and give them his ideas for future episodes. Each story idea was then sent to Hitchcock himself. If he didn't like an idea, he killed it then and there. If the director liked a story, he gave producers an immediate go-ahead.

Hitchcock liked Ray's ideas. The great director felt privileged to have a writer of Ray's stature contributing to his television show. Ray found Hitchcock to be a kind and gentle person with a good sense of humor. It was quite a change from working with John Huston.

Ray wrote seven teleplays for Hitchcock between 1955 and 1964, but he missed his big opportunity to work on one of the director's most famous movies. One day, Hitchcock gave Ray a copy of a short story by Daphne Du Maurier called "The Birds." He wanted to make the story into a movie, and he wanted Ray to write the screenplay.

> **"The film [*The Birds*] is full of holes. It's too long. Still, I often wonder what would have happened if I had written it. The ending of the film as it stands is very unsatisfactory."**
>
> – RAY BRADBURY

"The Birds" is a horror story about a mass attack by birds against humans in a small town. After Ray read the story, he told Hitchcock he would like to take the job. There was just one problem. Ray said he couldn't start working for two weeks. He was writing a teleplay for *Alfred Hitchcock Presents* at the time, and he had to finish that project before starting another. The director was unwilling to wait that long, so he gave the job to someone else. The movie was a smash hit and was nominated for several Academy Awards. "I should have done it," Ray said years later. "The film is full of holes. It's too long. Still, I often wonder what would have happened if I had written it. The ending of the film as it stands is very unsatisfactory."

## A VISIT TO GREEN TOWN

While he was writing for Hitchcock, Ray was also busy putting together his next book. The theme this time was not Mars or dinosaurs, but life as Ray experienced it in Waukegan in the year 1928. The title was to be *Dandelion Wine*. In the book, Waukegan would be called "Green Town."

In the book, Ray re-created a time past as seen through the eyes of a 12-year-old boy named Douglas Spaulding. The character is a thinly veiled version of Ray as a boy. (Douglas is Ray's actual middle name. Spaulding is Ray's father's middle name.) Each of the 40 short chapters in the book is loosely connected to a theme of a summer long ago. They present a picture of small-town life touched with dreams and fantasy, such as an attempt to build a "happiness machine" that backfires. Douglas's relationship with his father and to the summer landscape of Green Town are important parts of all the stories. Both are reflected in this passage:

> *And they walked through the forest, Father very tall,*
> *Douglas moving in his shadow, and Tom very small,*
> *trotting in his brother's shade. They came to a little*
> *rise and looked ahead. Here, here, did they see? Father*
> *pointed. Here was where the big summer-quiet winds*
> *lived and passed in the green depths, like ghost-*
> *whales, unseen.*

*Dandelion Wine* was published in September 1957. At the same time, Ray's father was admitted to a hospital. Leo had to share a hospital room with several other people. Ray wanted his

*Ray's mother always encouraged and supported his dreams of becoming a writer. The two enjoyed a very close relationship.*

father to have a private room, so he had him moved to Santa Monica Hospital. Two days later, Leo suffered a massive stroke. For two weeks, Ray visited his father twice a day, every day. Sadly, Leo never recovered. He died on October 20, 1957. Ray, his mother, and his brother, Skip, were devastated.

After Leo's death, Ray found comfort once again in his work and the vast world of his unique imagination. He continued working each day, turning out a short story a week, and coming up with plans for more stories, plays, scripts, and novels. Ray also found comfort in the newest addition to his family. Daughter Alexandra Allison Bradbury, soon to be known as "Zana," was born on August 13, 1958. Once again, the Bradbury family had outgrown their home. Ray and Maggie moved into a nearby three-bedroom house on Thanksgiving Day.

## ENTERING THE TWILIGHT ZONE

In early 1959, Ray was approached by a young television writer named Rod Serling. He told Ray that he wanted to create a television series called *The Twilight Zone*. The weekly show would feature fantasy dramas.

"Rod told me that he was starting a fantasy series," recalled Ray, "but he didn't really know what he was doing." The way

*Rod Serling was a busy man in the 1950s and 1960s. During that time, he wrote most of the scripts for* The Twilight Zone *and penned dozens of other teleplays.*

## The Twilight Zone

The Twilight Zone, which ran from 1959 to 1964, was one of the most popular science-fiction and fantasy television shows of all time. Each episode of the series presented viewers with an original story that almost always ended with a surprise twist. The writers who contributed to the show, including Ray Bradbury, used fantasy and science fiction to comment on current social problems or eternal human dilemmas. Frequent themes included nuclear war, racial prejudice, and greed. Although the series ended in 1964, The Twilight Zone can still be seen today in reruns.

Ray tells the story, he invited Serling over to his house. The two writers met in Ray's basement, and Bradbury gave Serling a pile of books by writers of dark fantasies. He even gave him some of his own books, including *The Martian Chronicles* and *Dandelion Wine*. Ray told him:

> *After you read these books you will have a complete idea of what your show should be like. Buy some of these stories or hire some of these authors to work for you, because you can't [write] the whole thing by yourself.*

Ray also agreed to be a regular contributor to *The Twilight Zone*. The first episode premiered on CBS on October 2, 1959. As he watched the program, Ray realized that the story—about an astronaut who wanders through a town looking for signs of life—was very similar to one of the stories in *The Martian Chronicles*. He was confused. He was sure that Serling wouldn't steal his work, yet he hadn't given the director permission to use the story.

A month later, Serling called Ray to apologize. He said that the story shown on *The Twilight Zone* was unconsciously based on "The Silent Towns" in *The Martian Chronicles*. Serling offered to pay Ray for using the story, but the author refused. "Let it go," he said. Despite noticing similarities between the fifth episode of *The Twilight Zone* and the images in *Dandelion Wine,* Ray went on to write three teleplays for Serling's show.

## SOMETHING WICKED

In 1959 Ray began work on his second novel, *Something Wicked This Way Comes*. The book is about two 13-year-old boys named Jim Nightshade and William Halloway. The boys encounter a strange lightning rod salesman who says that a storm is coming. Later, they see a poster for Cooger and Dark's Pandemonium Shadow Show. The traveling carnival rumbles into town at the darkest hour of 3 A.M., bringing "something wicked" with it. The evil carnival, around which the action of the novel takes place, menaces the boys with dark magic, a carousel that makes time go backward and forward, and magical mirrors that distort reality. The cast of characters includes an illustrated man, whose entire body is covered in tattoos, a mysterious "dust witch," and even Mr. Electrico, the strange character from Ray's own childhood.

Something Wicked This Way Comes *is one of Ray's scariest creations. He also wrote the screenplay for the 1983 movie adaptation of the book.*

*Something Wicked This Way Comes* proved to be one of Bradbury's most popular books. Other authors, such as Stephen King, say it influenced their writing. The novel was made into a movie, a play, and even inspired the theme for a *Simpsons* Halloween special. ❖

By the 1970s, Ray had already become a superstar among American writers. Still, he never stopped looking for new worlds to conquer.

CHAPTER NINE

# The Old Master

I N August 1972, ray published a children's
book called *The Halloween Tree*. It is one of the few books
that the author has written specifically for kids. It's about
his favorite holiday.

Ray always treasured Halloween when he was growing up in
Waukegan. He and his brother Skip would pile into Aunt Neva's
Model T Ford and ride west into the farm country to collect
pumpkins and dried corn for decorations. After he had a family
of his own, Ray created new traditions. He and Maggie would
combine Halloween and daughter Susan's birthday into one big
celebration. That evening, Ray would put on a mask and take
the girls trick-or-treating. Every year without fail, the girls would
find their candy stores mysteriously diminished when they woke
up the next morning. Ray always raided the girls' stash, while
they slept, and picked out his favorites.

The holiday Ray presented in *The Halloween Tree* hardly featured such good-natured fun. In the book, eight young boys gather to go trick-or-treating. One of the boys, named Pipkin, disappears. The others go to a haunted house, where there is a huge tree hung with jack-o'-lanterns. It is the Halloween tree. Pipkin appears nearby but is quickly carried away into the darkness. To help save him, the boys take a trip through time and space to discover the origins of Halloween. *The Halloween Tree* was made into an animated television special that aired on the Cartoon Network in 1993. Ray was the voice of the narrator. He also wrote the script—and won an Emmy Award for his work.

*Ray had long been a fan of Walt Disney's work. He was happy to participate in the planning of EPCOT and to help celebrate the company's 50th anniversary.*

## EPCOT

The Experimental Prototype Community of Tomorrow (EPCOT) was conceived by Walt Disney. When it was built, EPCOT was based on the latest ideas about how technology would shape the future. Today, EPCOT consists of two themed areas. Future World features attractions that focus on energy, communications, the environment, the ocean, transportation, and space exploration. World Showcase presents a series of foreign country exhibits that are set around a lagoon.

## WORKING FOR DISNEY

In 1976, Ray was hired to consult on the construction of Disney's EPCOT center. Executives at the company remembered that Ray had written a short program for the top floor of the U.S. pavilion at the 1964 World's Fair on Long Island, New York. It was an overview of U.S. history titled "The American Journey." Visitors were carried along a moving platform past movie screens. Each screen told part of the American story according to Ray's narration. The Disney executives also knew that shortly before his death, Walt Disney had struck up a friendship with Ray. Disney was a big fan of Ray's work, and the writer admired Disney's own creative genius. It seemed right that Disney executives now asked Ray to write the script for the main exhibit at EPCOT. After a few weeks, Ray completed a script for "Spaceship Earth." For this journey through the history of Earth, he envisioned a sound and light show that moved from early cave drawings all the way into the space age.

EPCOT was finally ready to open six years later in 1982. Ray boarded a train for a cross-country trip to attend the official

*Ray took great pride in every detail of* The Ray Bradbury Theater *and could frequently be found on the set. The author had an incredible amount of control over the show—he was the writer, executive producer, and host.*

opening in Orlando. The journey was like a nightmare from one of his stories. Ray was stranded in New Orleans, where he learned that there was no train service to Orlando. He hired a limousine to take him the 500 miles (805 kilometers) from New Orleans to Orlando. Then, somewhere in Florida, the limousine blew a tire—and the spare was no good! Ray and the driver walked down the highway to get a new tire. The driver put the new tire on and continued down the highway. That's when the car engine blew. With few other options left to them, Ray and the driver walked to a motel to spend the night. The next day, Ray paid a taxi driver to take him the rest of the way. Surprisingly, Ray managed to make the grand opening at EPCOT.

When the celebration was over, Ray found out there was no direct rail connection from Orlando to Los Angeles. He made a fateful decision: He would fly home. Although he spent the entire journey gritting his teeth and clutching the armrests, Ray never shied away from air travel after that first flight.

## THE RAY BRADBURY THEATER

In 1984, executives from Home Box Office (HBO) approached Ray with an idea for a show. It was a great deal for Ray. He would be sole writer and executive producer, and all the episodes would be based on his stories. He would also be the host. At the beginning of each episode, Ray would appear and introduce the program with these words:

*People ask, 'Where do you get your ideas?' Well, right here. All this is my Martian landscape. Somewhere in this room is an African veldt. Just beyond, perhaps, is a small Illinois town where I grew up. And I'm surrounded on every side by my Magician's toyshop. I'll never starve here. I just look around, find what I need, and begin. I'm Ray Bradbury, and this is* The Ray Bradbury Theater.

The first episode premiered on HBO on May 21, 1985. After six episodes, *The Ray Bradbury Theater* moved to the USA Network, where it stayed for the remainder of its seven-year run. Ray was involved in every aspect of the show. He even visited the sets on location. Yet he still wrote every day and produced a short story every week.

*On November 15, 2000, Ray attended the National Book Awards dinner in New York. He received the Medal for Distinguished Contribution to American Letters.*

Throughout the 1990s, Ray's fame grew even more. His writings had been translated into more than 20 foreign languages. He regularly found his works sharing shelf space with authors who were his childhood heroes: L. Frank Baum, Jules Verne, Edgar Rice Burroughs, and Edgar Allen Poe.

## TRIALS AND TRIUMPHS

On November 4, 1999, Ray was working at his vacation home in Palm Springs, California, when he suddenly went numb all over. He'd had a stroke. Luckily, Ray's limousine driver was there to take him to the hospital. From there he was transported back to Los Angeles. After a month, Ray was released from the hospital. He had lost 62 pounds (28 kilograms), but he was happy about it. "The whole experience has been good for me," he joked. "My blood pressure is normal again after years."

Once he got home, Ray worked to regain his strength. He progressed from a wheelchair to a walker to a cane. Through it all he never stopped writing.

In November 2000, Ray went to New York to receive the Medal for Distinguished Contribution to American Letters from the National Book Foundation. Maggie, who was not feeling well, stayed home. At the awards dinner the host—writer and actor Steve Martin—introduced Ray with these words:

*Novelist, short-story writer, essayist, playwright, screenwriter, and poet ... how can we even begin to count all of the ways in which Ray Bradbury has etched his indelible impressions upon the American literary landscape? There are few modern authors who can claim such a wide and varied provenance for their work, spanning from the secret inner-worlds of childhood dreams, to the magic realism of everyday life, to the infinite expanses of outer space.*

Ray was helped to the podium to deliver his acceptance speech. A week earlier, he had suffered another stroke that caused him to lose vision in his left eye. He said, in part:

*This is incredible. This is quite amazing because who you're honoring tonight is not only myself but the ghost of a lot of your favorite writers. And I wouldn't be here except that they spoke to me in the library. The library's been the center of my life. I never made it to college. I started going to the library when I graduated from high*

## The National Book Awards

The National Book Awards are among the top literary prizes in the United States. Awards are given for literature published in the previous year, as well as lifetime achievement awards such as the Medal for Distinguished Contribution to American Letters that was given to Ray Bradbury. Other recent recipients of this award include authors Toni Morrison, John Updike, Norman Mailer, and Arthur Miller.

*school. I went to the library every day for three or four days a week for 10 years and I graduated from the library when I was 28.*

*I have never been jealous or envious of other writers. I have been in love with them and my dream always was that some day I could go to the library and look up on the shelf and see my own name gleaming against L. Frank Baum and the wonderful Oz books, or against Edgar Allen Poe's or leaning against many other similar writers and knowing that Jules Verne was on a shelf down below me along with H. G. Wells. These are all my companions.*

When Ray finished speaking, he received a standing ovation. Even better than the audience acclaim was the knowledge that Ray's greatest dreams had come true in his lifetime. His more than 500 short stories, novels, plays, and poems now sit on the shelves of every library and bookstore along with those of other famous writers. Just as those writers influenced him, Ray's work has influenced a host of modern artists, from writer R. L. Stine to award-winning filmmaker Steven Spielberg.

"When I visit schools, kids always ask me 'What's the scariest book you've ever read?'" says Stine, "and I always tell them *Something Wicked This Way Comes.* I still remember how creepy it was. It really struck a chord with me."

After the ceremony, Ray returned to Los Angeles. He was happy to get back to his home, his wife, and his regular routine. Ray's peace was short-lived, though.

In the first few months of 2003, Maggie's strength seemed to give out. She rarely left the house anymore. Finally, when Maggie refused to get out of bed, Ray took her to the hospital. The diagnosis was not good: Maggie had advanced lung cancer. She died on November 24, 2003. Ray and Maggie had been married for 57 years. She had been his best friend, inspiration, and constant companion.

Nearly one year to the day that he lost his wife, on November 17, 2004, Ray traveled to Washington, D.C. He was being presented with the National Medal of Arts—the highest national honor given to artists by the United States government.

*Ray's studio is filled with books, papers, mementos, toys—all sorts of interesting objects—and, of course, a typewriter.*

Ray felt that everyone around him was dying, but he also felt that, when his turn came, he would live on through his works. Mr. Electrico was right when he told young Ray that he would live forever. Just as he had all those years ago, the writer still believed in Mr. Electrico's prediction. That evening, as he accepted his award, Ray said:

*The thing that makes me happy is that I know that on Mars, two hundred years from now, my books are going to be read. They'll be up on dead Mars with no atmosphere. And late at night, with a flashlight, some little boy is going to peek under the covers and read* The Martian Chronicles *on Mars.* ❖

# TIME LINE

**1920**  Ray Douglas Bradbury is born on August 22 in Waukegan, Illinois.

**1923**  Ray sees the film *The Hunchback of Notre Dame*, which leaves a huge impression on him.

**1926**  The Bradburys move to Tucson, Arizona.

**1927**  Ray and his family return to Waukegan.

**1928**  Ray is introduced to *Buck Rogers*, *Tarzan*, and *John Carter: Warlord of Mars*. He becomes fascinated by Mars and the world of fantasy.

**1932**  Ray meets Mr. Electrico, a magician who tells the boy he will live forever. Soon after, the Bradburys move back to Tucson.

**1933**  The family heads back to Waukegan.

**1934**  The Bradburys move to Los Angeles. Ray spends his free time writing radio scripts and trying to get autographs from his favorite stars.

**1936**  Ray joins the L.A. Science Fiction League, where he meets other future science-fiction greats, including Robert Heinlein and Forrest J. Ackerman.

**1939**  Ray attends the first-ever sci-fi convention on July 2 and 3 and visits the World's Fair.

**1941** Ray's story "Pendulum" is published in *Super Science Stories,* a pulp magazine.

**1947** *Dark Carnival,* Ray's first collection of stories, is published; he marries Marguerite (Maggie) McClure on September 27.

**1949** Ray's first daughter, Susan Marguerite, is born on November 5.

**1950** *The Martian Chronicles* is published. The collection of short stories is centered around an Earthling invasion of Mars.

**1951** *The Illustrated Man,* a collection of short stories, is published. Ray's daughter Ramona Anne is born on May 17.

**1953** In September, Ray begins work on the screenplay for *Moby Dick.* His first novel, *Fahrenheit 451,* is published.

**1955** Ray begins writing teleplays for *Alfred Hitchcock Presents.* His daughter Bettina Francion is born on July 22.

**1957** Ray's novel *Dandelion Wine* is published in September; Ray's father dies on October 20.

**1958** Alexandra Allison, Ray's third daughter, is born on August 13.

**1962** *Something Wicked This Way Comes,* a novel, is published.

**1964** Ray creates a screenplay for the U.S. pavilion at the New York World's Fair.

**1972** *The Halloween Tree,* Ray's first children's book, is published.

**1976** Ray consults on construction of EPCOT.

**1980** *The Martian Chronicles* airs on NBC.

**1983** The film version of *Something Wicked This Way Comes* is released.

**1985** HBO airs *The Ray Bradbury Theater.*

**1988-1992** *The Ray Bradbury Theater* airs on the USA Network.

**1999** Ray suffers his first stroke on November 4.

**2000** Ray receives the National Book Foundation's Medal for Distinguished Contribution to American Letters.

**2003** Ray's wife Maggie dies on November 24.

**2004** Ray receives the National Medal of Arts on November 17.

**2008** Ray attends the 13th annual *Los Angeles Times* Festival of Books.

# A CONVERSATION WITH
# *R. L. Stine*

*R. L. Stine is one of the best-selling children's authors of all time. He started writing stories and jokes—which he would hand out at school—when he was just 9 years old. Stine grew up in Ohio, a setting that finds its way into many of his stories. Here the author of the popular* Goosebumps *and* Rotten School *series talks about how Ray Bradbury influenced his life and work.*

**Q:** When you were growing up, did Ray Bradbury's writings influence you? How?

**A:** When I was 9 or 10 years old, I discovered his short stories. Up till then, I'd been reading mainly EC horror comics and *MAD* magazine. Bradbury's stories turned me into an avid reader. I couldn't believe how beautiful the language was—and the wonderful surprise endings.

**Q:** What is your favorite Ray Bradbury work, and why?

**A:** *Dandelion Wine.* I think this is one of the most underrated books of all time. I read it once a year. What a beautiful depiction of a time long gone. Every page is filled with such sadness and beauty.

**Q:** In what ways do you think Ray Bradbury influenced popular imagination in America?

**A:** *The Martian Chronicles* changed science-fiction writing forever. It … led to much more sophisticated plotting and characterization.

**Q:** You are quoted as saying that *Something Wicked This Way Comes* by Ray Bradbury was the scariest book you ever read. At what age did you read it, and how do you think it influenced your own writing, if it did?

**A:** I read it when it first came out in '62. I was 19. I already knew I wanted to be a writer. I identified with the Midwestern boys, coming as I did from Ohio. And it made me realize how important close point of view is in creating scares in a book. It was a lesson I try to remember every time I sit down to write.

**Q:** Bradbury says he was greatly influenced by the movies, comic strips, radio drama, and by the classics of children's literature. Do you think if he had grown up in today's world of television, video games, and the Internet, Ray would have produced the same body of work?

**A:** Yes, he might have created even more works since all of these platforms today require "content … content … content." There are even more outlets for someone with his amazing creativity.

**Q:** What do you think is Ray Bradbury's single most important strength as a writer?

**A:** No one writes like him. You always know it's a Bradbury story. His style is unique. It can't be copied.

**Q:** How has Ray Bradbury influenced your own writing?

**A:** I try to lure the readers into the story, as Bradbury does, with good storytelling and lots of twists and surprises.

**Q:** Do you think Bradbury's works will be as popular 50 years from now as they are today? If so, why?

**A:** Yes. Good storytelling like Ray's will always be popular. People live for stories. Everyone wants to know "what happens next?"

# GLOSSARY

**agent:** someone who is authorized to act on behalf of an artist, such as a writer or an actor

**allegation:** an unproven charge or reason

**anecdote:** a short item of amusing or biographical interest

**anthology:** a collection of selected pieces of art or writing

**bizarre:** strikingly out of the ordinary

**boisterous:** marked by excessive high spirits

**cataclysmic:** an event that brings great change

**catapulting:** jumping out quickly and violently

**closure:** the act of closing the action, as in a story plot

**consigned:** sent to an agent to be taken care of or sold

**crystalline:** strikingly clear or sparkling

**dilemma:** a situation involving a choice, usually between two actions

**enthralled:** held spellbound or in a trance

**fantasy:** fiction that features especially strange settings and characters

**fount:** a fountain or source of something

**handbill:** a small printed advertising sheet distributed by hand

**illusion:** a false perception of reality; a magic trick

**indelible:** cannot be erased, removed, or washed away

**migraine:** a condition marked by frequent severe headaches, often accompanied by nausea and vomiting

**parched:** deprived of natural moisture

**perplexed:** filled with uncertainty, puzzled

**precipitant:** condition of falling suddenly

**provenance:** origin or source

**pulp magazine:** an inexpensive magazine printed on cheap paper

**rousing:** brisk and lively

**science fiction:** fiction that deals with the impact of real or imagined science on society

**syndicate:** a business concern that sells materials for publication in a number of newspapers or other publications simultaneously

**technique:** a method of accomplishing a desired aim

**teleplay:** a play or program written for television

**torment:** to cause severe or recurrent distress or pain

**troupe:** a group of theatrical performers

**veldt:** a grassland, especially of southern Africa, with few bushes or trees

**vintage:** classic or typical

**zeal:** eagerness in pursuit of something; passion

# FOR MORE INFORMATION

## BOOKS AND OTHER RESOURCES

Aggelis, Steven L., ed. *Conversations with Ray Bradbury*. Jackson, Mississippi: University of Mississippi Press, 2004.

Bradbury, Ray. *Bradbury Speaks*. New York: William Morrow, 2005.

Weller, Sam. *The Bradbury Chronicles: The Life of Ray Bradbury*. New York: William Morrow, 2005.

*Ray Bradbury: An American Icon*. Monterey Video, 2007.

*Ray Bradbury: Story of a Writer*. American Film Foundation, 2004.

## WEB SITES

**Ray Bradbury**
**www.raybradbury.com**

This web site includes lots of facts about Ray's books, his life, and the philosophy behind his writing.

**Space Age City**
**www.spaceagecity.com/bradbury**

This site offers a biography of the author, as well as images and quotes from Ray. It also includes a list of his works in books, film, and television.

Publisher's Note: Our editors have carefully reviewed these recommended web sites, but we cannot guarantee that a site's future contents will continue to meet our high standards of quality and educational value. The publisher does not have any control over and does not assume any responsibility for third-party web sites.

# SELECT BIBLIOGRAPHY AND SOURCE NOTES

Bradbury, Ray. *From the Dust Returned*. N.Y.: William Morrow, 2002.

Bradbury, Ray. *The Martian Chronicles*. N.Y.: Bantam Books, 1979.

Bradbury, Ray. *Vintage Bradbury*. N.Y.: William Morrow, 1990.

Eller, Jonathan R., and William F. Touponce. *Ray Bradbury: The Life of Fiction*. Kent, Ohio: Kent State University Press, 2004.

Weller, Sam. *The Bradbury Chronicles*. N.Y.: William Morrow, 2005.

## PAGE 2

*The Washington Times*. January 1, 2006

## CHAPTER ONE

Page 8, line 5: Weller, Sam. *The Bradbury Chronicles*. N.Y.: William Morrow, 2005, p. 56
Page 9, line 6: Ibid.
Page 9, line 20: Eller, Jonathan R., and William F. Touponce. *Ray Bradbury: The Life of Fiction*. Kent, Ohio: Kent State University Press, 2004, p. 15
Page 10, line 3: Ibid.
Page 11, line 4: Weller, p. 11

## CHAPTER TWO

Page 13, line 13: Weller, pp. 11–12
Page 14, line 9: Nevins, Winfield. *The Salem Trials*. Salem, Mass.: Salem Press Company, 1916, p. 212
Page 16, line 11: Weller, p.25
Page 17, line 9: Ibid., p. 26
Page 17, line 20: Ibid., p. 28
Page 18, line 10: Ibid., p. 30

Page 22, line 1: Ibid., p. 41
Page 23, line 12: Ibid., p. 44
Page 23, line 23: Ibid.
Page 24, line 11: Ibid., p. 48

## CHAPTER THREE

Page 31, line 15: Weller, p. 74
Page 32, line 3: Ibid.
Page 32, line 26: Ibid.
Page 35, line 12: Ibid., p. 82

## CHAPTER FOUR

Page 38, line 1: Weller, p. 85
Page 39, sidebar: Ibid., p. 89
Page 41, line 9: Ibid., p. 97

## CHAPTER FIVE

Page 49, line 7: Weller, p. 125
Page 51, line 4: Bradbury, Ray. *From the Dust Returned*. N.Y.: William Morrow, 2000, p. 125
Page 56, line 3: Bradbury, Ray. *The Martian Chronicles*. N.Y.: Bantam Books, 1979, p. 2
Page 57, line 9: Asimov, Isaac. *Asimov on Science Fiction*. N.Y.: HarperCollins Publishers, 1983, p. 110

## CHAPTER SIX

Page 59, line 7: Weller, p. 167
Page 60, line 7: Bradbury, Ray. "The Foghorn." *Vintage Bradbury*. N.Y.: William Morrow, 1990, p. 269
Page 63, line 4: Weller, pp. 199–200
Page 65, line 18: Ibid., pp. 205–206
Page 66, line 6: Prescott, Orville. "Books of the Times." *The New York Times*, October 15, 1953
Page 66, sidebar: WorldNetDaily, posted June 3, 2004

## CHAPTER SEVEN

Page 69, line 11: Weller, p. 161
Page 70, line 11: Ibid., p. 210
Page 72, line 7: Ibid., p. 223
Page 73, line 18: Ibid.

## CHAPTER EIGHT

Page 79, line 25: Weller, p. 238
Page 80, line 18: Bradbury, Ray.
    "Dandelion Wine." *Vintage
    Bradbury*, p. 198
Page 82, line 9: Weller, p. 251
Page 83, line 6: Ibid., p. 253
Page 84, line 10: Ibid.

## CHAPTER NINE

Page 91, line 25: http://www.
    innermind.com/myguides/guides/
    bradbury/htm
Page 93, line 13: Weller, p. 238
Page 93, line 23: http://
    www.nationalbook.org/
    nbaacceptspeech_rbradbury_intro.
    html
Page 94, line 9: http://www.
    nationalbook.org/
    nbaacceptspeech_rbradbury.html
Page 95, line 20: Weller, p. 249
Page 97, line 7: Weller, Sam. "Semper
    Sci Fi." *Chicago Tribune
    Magazine*, August 13, 2000

# INDEX

# ABOUT THE AUTHOR

Charles Piddock is a former editor in chief of Weekly Reader Corporation, which publishes classroom magazines for schools from pre-K through high school—including *Current Events* and *Current Science*. In his career with Weekly Reader, he has written and edited hundreds of articles for young people of all ages on world and national affairs, science, literature, and other topics. Before working at Weekly Reader, he worked in publishing in New York City, and, before that, served as a Peace Corps volunteer in rural West Bengal, India.

## PICTURE CREDITS